THE SPIRITUAL TRAVELLER'S GUIDEBOOK TO ETERNITY

The Goddess

By Nolan Luke
(Narendar Puri)Naga Baba

VOL. I
PART 3

First Edition

Copyright © 2017 by Nolan Luke

All rights reserved. This book may not be reproduced in whole or in part, stored in a retrieval system or transmitted in any form or by any means; mechanical, electronic or any other; without written permission from the publisher, except by a reviewer, who may quote brief passages in a review.

Names have been changed in respect to individual privacy. Actual names are stated with love.

Published by
Transalaya, Inc./Transalaya Publishing
P.O. Box 1177
Baldwin Park, CA 91706

First Printing
ISBN 978-0-9989025-4-8

CONTENTS

Chapter 1   The Formless – The Goddess Seen   P 2

- Two Independent Individuals
- There and Here Now
- Naked Beauty
- The Blue Star Light Orchestra
- The Formless
- Go No Further
- Contemplation
- Caravan Night
- The Goddess
- Escort for Beauty
- Pretty One
- The Goddess Blessed Me
- Memories
- Love and Blessings to Mahant Rampuri
- On the Way to Formlessness
- Sight of the Goddess
- Untitled
- The Goddess in Her Shower
- Beauty
- How Much Love
- A Wish

Chapter 2   The Goddess   P 49

Caregiving
The Goddess Again
The Goddess I See in You
The Goddess Goes for Her Evening Bath
The Formless Isness Within the Goddess
The Goddess Was Worshipped Long Before God was Worshipped
The Goddess in Her Naked Form
I Dreamed I held the Goddess
The Goddess Steps into View
The Goddess Body Form
The Goddess Gave Birth to Shiva
The Goddess in Her Shrine
The Goddess in Your Eyes

Chapter 3 The Creator   P 100

Beauty Personified
The Creator   I
The Creator II
III
IV
Siren Call
She Touched Me

A Direct Call from Sach Khand
The Isness
The True Reflection of Formless Spirit
The Unmanifest Isness

Chapter 4   My Beloved – The Singularity – Goddess Mookambika   P127

My Beloved Said
  I Looked at Beauty
  I Should Not Write Down
  That Formless Singularity
  When I Was a Kid
  Formless Spirit
  Just Below the Surface
 Just Six Seconds Away
  Love Freedom and Liberty
  The Goddess Mookambika
  Mental Focus
  Spirit
  The Shabdanam
  The One Divinity
  We Learn God Is Love
  Eternity
  A Dive into Nothingness
  Spirit Lifetime
  Beauty

Spiritual Imagery
Into the Wind
The Daughter
The Box
The Airey Tale
The Breezes Pass By
The Goddess

Chapter 5 The Physical material – Liberation – Reincarnation   P 189

A Butterfly
Samadhi
The Squirrel Existential Leap
The Dance of Liberation
Lifetime After Lifetime
Divine Mother
Rain

By Nolan Luke, (Narendar Puri)Naga Baba

CHAPTER ONE

THE FORMLESS –
THE GODDESS SEEN

TWO INDEPENDENT INDIVIDUALS

We were two independent individuals
In a love state relationship
We each liked and needed alone time and space daily
We enjoyed the pleasure of meeting each day
We looked forward to seeing each other
When together
Most of the time we were embracing and kissing
Hours could go by unnoticed
We could easily spend all day together
And stay up all night talking
We were great together in small places
For long periods of time
We touched kissing and embracing every day
We both used the Inner
We both pursued spiritual liberation this lifetime
We made each other happy and laugh
I would do anything for her
She would do anything for me
We each loved our Guru Paul Twitchell first
We each loved The Creator second
We loved each other third
We thus discovered the love of Guru and God inside of the other
Other than work and work related activities duties and events
We chose to spend time together
We also did things apart
We both regretted ever the rare disagreement
We did not let either ego enter into our relationship

By Nolan Luke, (Narendar Puri)Naga Baba

THERE AND HERE NOW

The Formless
Is a destination
Beyond name form sight and visibility

No need to go there
No need to go there now

Eternity and infinity the start
Should be enough

The journey is an ordeal
Distractions all along the way

The qualities and aspects of GOD abound
Throughout the God worlds and eternity

These same qualities can be found
In true light Gurus and Masters

We can travel far country horizons
Across Creation itself

And still find GOD within a true Guru
Seeing and being seen in the Darshan

The truth is the living light and voice of GOD
On earth as it is also in the heavens above
7-17-13

By Nolan Luke, (Narendar Puri)Naga Baba

NAKED BEAUTY

I looked up and there she was
As always her eyes held me paralyzed
I could not move
I could barely breathe
I forgot my name
I lost track of time
I stood in timelessness

I could only smile
I was staring at Beauty
Up close
Her face her eyes her lips
I leaned towards her
I retreated
Discipline I must above all be disciplined
So I step backwards
As if in time

I see a vision before me
Beautiful body
Shy
She wears only a modest smile
To hide behind
Naked beauty
Naked truth
The Grail of any true mystic or spiritual quest
Abstractions in the flesh

Warm and vibrant
I would wish to touch softly her face
Across time and space
7-17-13

By Nolan Luke, (Narendar Puri)Naga Baba

THE BLUE STAR LIGHT ORCHESTRA

Diane Gail
Performs
With the Blue Star Light Orchestra
On the outdoor stage
Just off the Main Floor
Of the Palace of the Sat Nam
In the Sach Khand Region
Of the Sat Lok Plane

It is a hundred and three piece orchestra
She will be conducting
From her harp at times
She will even be singing

There are her original creative pieces
Works she practiced while here on earth

I recognized her riffs
Heard them as she conceived them
The creativity of sound
The correspondence to color
The correlation to perfume and scent
Each note a chord
Each chord a show of color frequencies
Vibrations and reverberations

I see hear and smell the intoxicating fragrances of
    songs she wrote in Covina
Now played in eternity
Me listening third row center seat
She is happy her light so bright I squint my eyes to
    see and hear
7-17-13

By Nolan Luke, (Narendar Puri)Naga Baba

THE FORMLESS

The Formless
Grants freedom freewill and choice to each and all
Though it wants each Soul to return home
IT gives freedom to each Soul to decide its own fate

The Formless
Beams Love unconditionally
While allowing permitting each Soul go its own way
The ultimate love
The ultimate detachment

The Formless
Is never known by all

The Formless
Is buffered and hidden by eternity

The Formless is still a secret in eternity
Its whereabouts are unknown

Looking for the Creator in eternity
Takes as much courage
As hunting for bear in bear country
The hunter can get eaten by the bear

When you finally arrive in Sat Nam's hall
Count your blessings you are home

By Nolan Luke, (Narendar Puri)Naga Baba

GO NO FURTHER

Unless you have business at the VORTEX
Immediately
Settle into the true form of light existence
The Soul form of Being
In the infinite realms of eternity
Where Form is visible and tactile
Features are distinct without decay
Forms on the Soul Plane
Are true real and solid to the touch
All kinds of Souls populate eternity
Everyone has a story or song to sing
Ask for all the Joy of Infinity lit skies
Lament and sorrow for Souls
Still in duality
Still in negative karma debt
Still swinging on the pendulum of time
The yin and yang the opposites the contradictions
The upsets the unexpected the reversals
Lament and sorrow for Souls
Still down in the material worlds
Reincarnating again and again
Almost remembering learning spiritual truth
When abruptly the lifetime ends
And Soul must start all over again
In a new birth and body
So individual Souls wait in eternity

For loved ones still in time
Subject to death and rebirth
7-17-13

By Nolan Luke, (Narendar Puri)Naga Baba

CONTEMPLATION

The Soul Consciousness advances
With spiritual practice
Spiritual exercises
Right attitude
Right attention

Contemplation
Opens the individual
To light sound truth love beauty and goodness

These absolutes of GOD
Are aspects of Soul

These are frequencies
Of the one same ISNESS

As one is filled with truth revealed
The heart is filled with love overflowing
Beauty and goodness fill the beingness
The light sound fills the awareness

The spiritually unaware
Is transformed
Into the selfless state of giving
Love that has been received
Into the love that is given

Material becomes spiritual
7-18-13

By Nolan Luke, (Narendar Puri)Naga Baba

CARAVAN NIGHT

Night has fallen
On the hot blazing Summer day

In an oasis
Under a palm date grove
We seated on the ground
Beside a pool of water
Fed by an underground spring

Desert nights are cool and cold
Insects stir the air
Attracted by our fires
The wind barely moves the smoke

Music music
Fingers rapidly slap a drum
A flute pipes a tune
A stringed instrument tunes up
Bells ring
Out of a tent a Dancer steps
With bells on her ankles and coins on her hips
Her eyes seared every man deep
To the Soul level
She danced into our dreams
Reminding us of loved ones waiting our return
Three more nights and we will be home
Forty-two days it has been

On this Camel Caravan to retrieve silks and perfumes
7-18-13

By Nolan Luke, (Narendar Puri)Naga Baba

THE GODDESS

A Daughter of the Goddess
She steps into her shower
A waterfall cascading down into a pool into a stream
Her hand reaches out to test the water
I see her disappear
Gone from view
Then a foot appears
Then a lovely curved calf and knee
Then the most sensual symmetry of thigh and hip
Emerges from the waterfall cascade
I see her face
She is beautiful
She is sublime
The world around me melts away
I look upon her contemplating
Seeing with the Third Eye
I see she giving me such a big smile
I open my physical eyes
But she is behind the waterfall
Just then a heel a shoulder come out of the water
My what a most exquisite derriere
As was the Goddess Venus of the ancient Greeks
So well endowed she was with an incredible perfect backside
That statues of her dotted the Mediterranean coasts

So too it appears the Goddess Mookambika
And the Kali Shadashi form of the Goddess
Has such a divinely magnificent derriere
I am gazing at timelessness
Beauty on earth as seen in heaven

By Nolan Luke, (Narendar Puri)Naga Baba

Where Beauty stands
Is hallowed ground of her temple
I witness her divine presence in my life
Heaven can wait
Yet heaven is here
The Divine Mother
The Triple Goddess Mookambika
Is already here in the manifest outer world
And the age we are in
Does bear her name
The Kaliyuga
The Iron Age of man
The Divine Mother
Steps into the outer world
Here in the Western countries
Where back in time
Before recorded time
The Triple Goddess
Was revered and worshiped world wide
Peace trade and commerce
Esoteric history calls it the Satya Yuga
The Golden Age of woman on earth
Now here in the last age in the Iron Age of man
Divine Mother
The Triple Goddess
Mookambika
Kali Shodashi
Reappears to be seen

I see her naked features
And it is as if I read her story already written
I hear her answers to questions I earlier asked
I see how truth and beauty enter the world
I see the Goddess viewing her own reflection

In my views of her
In my mind's eye
In my closed eyes open third eye
In my open eyes on the outer world
I see abstract truths revealed in her female form
Why do you think the ancients
Saw their Goddesses and Gods nude
Because naked truth naked beauty naked goodness
Reveals clues nuances and knowledge
To the Intuition and the mind
The light of a Goddess seen without costume
Enlightens the mind opens the heart
For here is the Goddess revealing herself
Here is the Temple space
So she is worshiped
With love
With pure love
With love naked
Love unconditionally
Love that is filled with joy laughter happiness
Love that liberates Soul out of body
Love that frees Soul to embrace the Divine

By Nolan Luke, (Narendar Puri)Naga Baba

I admit I did at one time
While in the Mookambika Temple
Obviously out of my correct mind
Wonder how did the Goddess
Look
You know
Naked without the new Sari
She got each day
It blurted forth before I could catch it
I expected the worst to happen to me
Instead I thought I heard a giggle
When it was my turn and I was before her
In her Inner Sanctum
I closed my eyes
And I for a moment thought I glimpsed her form
She was beautiful
I felt embarrassed
She laughed
I was hooked
Reeled in and simply put in a basket
Such encounters occurred in ancient times
Such encounters still occur
But then
I look back through my lifetime backwards
And I see her always there in the picture
Who knows
Perhaps I was hers before I got here
7-20-13

ESCORT FOR BEAUTY

I am a good escort for beauty
I remember one time
Diane and I went to dinner at Chambord
After attending a Play

A guy comes over to our table
And says
I told my wife if this woman you are with
Will leave with me I am leaving her
Diane smiled and graciously declined
He turned to me and said
I hope you know you are a lucky man
I smiled and nodded

We were still there when they left their table
They were arm in arm smiling

Diane and I knew they were going to have a great
 evening

It is the beauty in art that makes it fine
Beauty transforms flesh and matter into spirit
The curator saves beauty by displaying beauty
The artist renders the beauty of vision
The sculptor uncovers the beauty in rock
The lover of beauty shares his discovery

By Nolan Luke, (Narendar Puri)Naga Baba

The Musician enacts the divine beauty of sound heard
Entrusted with beauty and still just a struggling poet
I pen my descriptions of her
That you experience your own direct contact with beauty
7-20-13

PRETTY ONE

Love dear love come closer to me
Pretty one come closer
Look me in the eye and smile
Entwine me with your arms
Listen
Do you hear my heart beating loudly
Above the quiet of the night
How can you hear clearly
Love dear love come closer still
Soul can you feel my heart in heaven
I see truth in your eyes
Tears wash your past incarnations
Suffering clouds lifetimes uncounted
Dim shadows hid the sun
Windowless rooms hid the moon
Your prayers and tearful pleas were heard
Yet so many lifetimes continued to pass
As if eleven thousand years unkissed
You soul sleeping since ancient goddess temple days
In a spell bound and gagged
You were seen and heard no more
Pretty one come closer
Let me see you
Through the light that is true unconditional

By Nolan Luke, (Narendar Puri)Naga Baba

THE GODDESS BLESSED ME

The Goddess blessed me
With the sight of you Diane Gail

I had been blinded by sorrow
Tears filled my vision

Then I saw you
I rubbed my eyes red not believing them

Then the Goddess spoke
With her sweetest voice

Judge her not by her spiritual experience or lack of
Follow my words and instruction
View her as already healed
See her according to her future destiny
Deep deep within her love is found
Her bodies are responsive to true love
Her heart needs love as electricity
Her skin craves the touch of Soul immaterial
Her lips are as if never kissed
She is only recently reborn soul
Her slate will be wiped clean
Of the pains sufferings and sacrifices of conditional love
She can take the love you have to give
Unconditional love turns her into beauty

The Goddess told me
Kiss her and she turns younger
Before your eyes
Give her her inner space
Often embrace and caress her body
Give her every kind of love unconditional
She is like a Goddess on earth
Be her mirror
Be truth
She needs and requires love
A priority in her existence

In union she will visit and see GOD
In love entwined she maintains free
Deeper in love she will be
She loves the Goddess more
She is a good love for you
For you both Guru God and Goddess
Come first in love prayer and devotion
Loving Soul to Soul in body
On every plane to each other
A dance together
That carriers both of you into the divine
Between you two divinity is in the touch
In her eyes you see Soul looking through
She is already awake
Help her get up

By Nolan Luke, (Narendar Puri)Naga Baba

MEMORIES

Sweet delicious juicy
Is the lush summer fruit
That is my love

Hot July is today
Ripe in mid season
She refreshes me

Her smooth skin
Excites all my nerve endings
Like a peach in hand
I almost squeeze too hard

From flesh so youthful
Full bosom breast
So pretty so sweet
Young and growing

Her body is going forward
Backward in time and years
Curvaceous lines being a smile

I feel I am captured
By her body
I surrender
I have no defense
I have no resistance

I see her naked
And know the Goddess
Is revealed
She permits me to see
Her sacred beingness
In the living form of Soul
In body she speaks to me
I speak to the body
I speak to the Goddess inside
I admit I stare at her beauty
Here I see all my desires
Beautiful face eye nose lips ears
A slender neck I long to kiss
Beautiful head to feet
A beautiful bottom
Such as to set my heart aflutter
Narrow waist sensuous hips
And legs so lovely
I clutch my throat
I can barely breathe
I see her all in one glance
I chew my fingernails
Ah
I may appear cool calm outside
Yet inside
The heart is racing
I am losing blood to the brain

By Nolan Luke, (Narendar Puri)Naga Baba

I am shallow breathing
Please don't call it panting
I am getting light-headed
She turns and I am hypnotized
I follow her every movement
Who can blame me
Many might envy me
I do not understand my luck
Of course this is my good fortune
But it is not Karma
It is Love
Love keeps us free
Love delivers us

LOVE AND BLESSING TO MAHANT RAMPURI

OM
Mahant Rampuri
My love and blessings to you on this very
special day. I bow before you. I thank
you for your love your presence and your
support these last few years. With your
continued help in so many forms I was able
to care for the love of my material life Diane Gail
every day in her final years.

You introduced me to the Divine Mother
Mookambika Goddess. I gained by the
service I did for Diane. I see that now.
Divine Mother embraced me and has not yet let go.

Diane passed late December 2012 and it has
taken until now to re-adjust to the world as
around me. I had to neglect almost everything
else in order to take good care of Diane I did.

I take this day to express my love to you and
request you excuse my absence. I see
it has been awhile. There is much I
neglected during this time. I am working to
return to being a support to you and your
efforts, soon.

I am much better now and am ready to pick

By Nolan Luke, (Narendar Puri)Naga Baba

up where we were last or to start from the
beginning. You Mahant Rampuri and Divine
Mother are a part of my daily life.

None of this has been easy and I got way behind on almost
everything. But I also saw what love and miracles
can do every day.   I learned to live life the day
as consciousness relating to consciousness.

I did not think it would take this long
to get over Diane's leaving. Big change. Readjusting.
Getting back to normal, steadily.

ON THE WAY TO FORMLESSNESS

When I am speaking to Soul Diane Gail
I am speaking to the Goddess within
The Kali Shodasi the Mookambika the Divine Mother
But Diane is Goddess
And may have been a living Goddess of a Temple before
Multiple lifetimes
Diane Gail
Goddess Love and Beauty
The material living light being
That will speak her heart with joy and happiness
The most direct means to enter the world
The Trinity of Goddesses
Though they come out of formlessness
They manifest in physical flesh
And walk the earth time to time
Today they walk the footsteps
Today they dance practice steps
Kali Shodasi dancing
Worshipped in her own inner sanctum
The Goddess
Is the very center of Tantra
Divine meditation on God
Divine meditation on Goddess
Focus on the Divine

By Nolan Luke, (Narendar Puri)Naga Baba

Attention on the Divine
Experiencing God and Goddess in form
On the way to Formlessness
Held in a sacred embrace
7-23-13

SIGHT OF THE GODDESS

The Goddess wants me to
Depict her as I see her
Describing her body form
She wants to hear
She loves how she looks
Hearing a sweet rendition of her beauty

Some South Indian poetry is steamy and lush
She has such a shape
To inspire such lines
She is Kali
She is the raving beauty
That saves the day
She is who will dance
She comes with work to do

Oh if I were to speak my heart
At the sight of the Goddess naked
The corners of the page would curl from the heat
Such beauty and truth is the Goddess
Such feminine endowment beauty and grace
Affects breathing
Imagination clouds my vision
Romance fills my ears
Such a beautiful gorgeous body
I am in love with beauty and truth
I love the woman by loving the Goddess

By Nolan Luke, (Narendar Puri)Naga Baba

I love the Goddess by loving the woman
Ultimately I be loving the Formless
In Its most beautiful and truthful forms
In creation
7-23-13

I nearly wept when I saw her breast
No fruit imagery here
No allegory no metaphor

Pretty perfect breast
I would wish to kiss
Though Goddess she be

By Nolan Luke, (Narendar Puri)Naga Baba

HER SHOWER I

Naked Goddess
Your skin glistens wet
Your hair shines
Your fingers touch my face

I see you up close
I see dimples
I see your skin pores

I try not to look at your breast
Pretty and near perfect

And all this time
I barely glanced down
To see your Goddess body bottom
I feared to see the Goddess Venus mound
I might wish to stand you on a pedestal
And pen an ancient ode to Beauty
Your beauty timeless in youth
Your shape and figure
Turns me into a wine sopped poet
The sweet feminine scent of your skin and hair
Affects me going backwards in time
How many lifetimes
You were the temple Goddess
You were the divine presence of the Goddess
You were her and she was you

HER SHOWER II

Today I see you blending unifying
When dancing you are at onement
Naked you become the Goddess entirely
Casting off the outer material layers
Naked you be truth unadorned

Naked you be the Goddess
In her temple
Dedicated to Love and Miracles
Teaching the power of love unconditional
While dancing the freedom that is truth
Sensuality and spirituality are the same
One is with form the other is without form
Sexuality becomes transmuted into love and beauty
Spirit going to God through the material
Love is a very expeditious path to GOD
Wise men and Poets have marked the way
But how much credit is given to the Goddess
The Divine Mother who gave the insight
The knowledge the wisdom and the poetry
She uses beauty to instruct on truth
In the open for all to see
But she instructs in private in the heart
Overnight I am filled with her love
I remember visiting no school
I remember only her grace and beauty

By Nolan Luke, (Narendar Puri)Naga Baba

To touch and embrace her
I receive an advanced degree
The study of the nameless formless Singularity
7-24-13

BEAUTY I

There is mortal prettiness
And then there is ecstatic beauty
Of the divine Goddess
Divine beauty is Truth
Truth is a divine abstract
That can be experienced in a divine beauty
Seen on earth in the Goddess
Beauty though immaterial
Manifests into our reality
That we know the living qualities and aspects
Of the Formless
The Goddess is that Formless ISNESS
Beyond adequate description
The Goddess in living body
Is a miracle out of love
Another immaterial aspect quality of the Formless
I see beauty of the Goddess before me
And I see the unseen revealed
I love her
Someone hear my plea
If I am not careful
I could come to desire her
Detachment detachment detachment
Divine mind reminds me
My nose and tongue trace the air

By Nolan Luke, (Narendar Puri)Naga Baba

Where she stood
Seeking a clue of her fragrance and taste

BEAUTY II

The Goddess beauty is timeless
She is every age of womanhood
Though she is ever in youth
Her naked beauty
Is like reading a book
On the making of creation
What god qualities are needed for manifestation
My eyes improved their vision and perception
Insight comes with its own light to see by
The Goddess is divine and is a woman
To be equally experienced
In the material worlds of duality

Duality has advantages to Soul
The Formless abstract invisible and immaterial
Can be seen and experienced
While wrapped in the arms of a woman
Touch taste and smell all give a clue
To the divinity within each Soul
The material reveals the sacred
Lovemaking remakes the cosmos
Puts Soul into the heavenly realms
Timeless passage in eternity
Love is Bhakti in any language
Love is an easy swing at evening

By Nolan Luke, (Narendar Puri)Naga Baba

Gliding between material and immaterial
The Goddess here beside me
7-25-13

HOW MUCH LOVE

My love
You have no idea

You have no idea
How much I love you

I don't care if you reside in eternity
I don't care if you live with the Goddesses

My Love
You have no idea

How much I truly love you
How much you ask

I love you all the way to God's open door

Me comfortable in your arms
We in our embrace

Carried home on the Bani wind
Such love divine is welcome in the presence of God

Let God witness our kiss on the doorstep
The Creator is the unseen hidden

By Nolan Luke, (Narendar Puri)Naga Baba

That mercifully acted on our behalf
That I find you with a heart of the Goddess
Your heart is connected to God
Thus I can love you all the way to God
7-25-13

A WISH

Maybe I brought all this on myself
When I said to the Goddess
In her Inner Sanctum
I would really love you if you were real
Oops
She stepped into manifestation

Be careful what you ask for
Goes the old saying

Well lucky me

Maybe she heard that as my wish
Good she did
But I was only thinking out loud

Images idols and statues
Do not normally come alive
Unless they are already alive

Those who visit her
Know she is living
She stands ready ever to protect and defend
But her heart is love
I should fear that she loves me

By Nolan Luke, (Narendar Puri)Naga Baba

But sometimes as now
With so much love between
Perhaps a little giddy
I go forth fearless
To live a truth uttered in true wishfulness
7-25-13

CHAPTER TWO

THE GODDESS

By Nolan Luke, (Narendar Puri)Naga Baba

CAREGIVING

Diane Gail
The time spent was much fun

Meeting you here in the physical material
That first physical sight of you
Reverberated like mystic inspired visions
In my head mind heart and body

I vibrate still in your glow
What a great light I see in you

From that first meeting
You never went away

We stayed young and fresh
That glimmer in the eye always there

We did not say goodbye
I just realized that this morning

We said I love you back and forth
We kissed I believe three times
We smiled
I gave you a sponge bath
Rolled you from your left side to your back
We made eye contact again we smiled
I picked up the basket and put it to the side
I looked back and you were gone

Almost every day for forty two years
We enjoyed and had the pleasure
Of each other's company
Spending time together
That may have been the most fun
We did really well together in tight places
No friction when our auras touched and overlapped
We got along enjoyably sharing the same aura bubble
I liked everything about you
Including the things that drove me up the wall
Like constantly being late to go somewhere
Yet when you did appear
Wow
We would be on Muse Goddess time
Perfect timing

Because you light up the room
With that smile and tilt of your head
Something happens to the person inside themselves
While all the clocks and watches disappear
Timelessness surrounds you
I notice it more since you left
You held the Inner worlds in your Third Eye
You say it all with a smile
And listened like a musician
Every topic was a treat
Especially where we disagreed
So all this is to say I miss you
And I am glad to have you by my side
7-28-13

By Nolan Luke, (Narendar Puri)Naga Baba

THE GODDESS AGAIN

The Temple attendant
Had closed off the shower area
My access to the Goddess
Her shrine
Closed from viewing

I did so miss
Watching her taking her showers divine
Her body beautiful sensual in grace
Raises my blood pressure
Elevates my thinking
Until I can only speak in poetry
How else can I describe her

In prose who will believe me
So the less words said the better
Can I out loud say what beauty I see

Can I truly relate the excitement I feel
Feeling the love she gives me
Her features looked at individually
Would be considered a fine art collection

She seen complete
Is woman on the verge of divine beauty

While the perfect aspect of woman
The Goddess materializes
Out of the mist
Beautiful I cannot take my eyes off her

I touch her to prove her real
My hand is wet and water sprinkles my page
Some of the ink runs and hides the words
Inspired by the vision of naked beauty
Revealing the unseen nature of truth
7-31-13

By Nolan Luke, (Narendar Puri)Naga Baba

She stayed in the shower of rain falling
Extra time this evening
Perhaps because the Temple was closed
These past many days

I was almost upset
With the Divine Mother

She had first given a tease
Later she gave a kiss a taste
Then she took all away

I almost said something
About rumors I have heard said
That Divine Mother often plays tricks
So maybe it could be true
Perhaps
But for now
Here I experience the Goddess
Everywhere she may be
And be unseen
But here in this breathing living temple
The Goddess I see and hear
As she truly catches my eye
For those long stares within
She sees me I see her
There is some unknown familiarity
I cannot yet explain
I barely understand it yet myself
Her skin is still wet
7-31-13

THE GODDESS I SEE IN YOU

The Goddess I see in you
I saw in my dream
I think she intends to step
Into our physical manifestation

In long ago centuries past
The Goddess did breathe and live
In the outer everyday world
Of men and women

In those long ago days
The living Goddesses
Lived in or near their temples

But these are not those days
We live in the Kali Yuga time

A Goddess living somewhere
Every lifetime since the beginning
Starting with the first early people of India
Every lifetime
A Goddess

A Goddess living
Not only left the district

By Nolan Luke, (Narendar Puri)Naga Baba

Of her temple
She left the State

She left the Indian subcontinent
She traveled abroad centuries ago

So in this lifetime
She would not know who she be
She always a little distant
She to the extreme
Disbelief her everyday theme
Often keeping to herself
Secrets and dreams
Too unbelievable to believe

The present day Goddess living
Is the Goddess still
Yet here she is
Divine yet in the world
Her light and beauty
Revealed in her eyes and material body

I am almost sure her body
Is a material body for the Goddess
Only aspects of her body have I seen
Feet ankles calves
Hands arms shoulders

By Nolan Luke, (Narendar Puri)Naga Baba

Waist torso belly button
Head neck and shoulders
Is all I have actually seen

Any more description
Is imagination extrapolation
And maybe wishful thinking

The water falling cascades
Such that she is obscured
By the spray and mist of the falls
And then she is covered in the towel
So you see my vision of her is limited
I stand so far away
Oh I would wish to stand closer
But I at least have this distant view

I have a time or two been very close
But the mist and water ruins the paper tablets
I write upon

So I must rely on hearsay other's writings
And old images and my impressions of her
To piece together my tellings of her
I have discussed this very topic today
With Divine Mother
The Poet needs to better see the Goddess
My mystic nature is born out of experience
First hand direct eye witness experience

I can verify she be the Goddess actual
I saw her etched on ancient temple walls
And the frescos depicting her naked
In her jewels and hip girdle
Like so many photos of her etched in stone
I memorized her beauty in my mind and heart
Such sensual divine beauty in this reality
I spend days revisiting those ruins
I copied those etchings into my mind
There I discovered for myself
Ideal beauty in a woman
Ideal beauty in a Goddess

Material beauty is often rare and fleeting
So it's carved into granite and stone
Held so that it be experienced
By a later viewer as was I in New Delhi
Beauty long gone for centuries
It is captured into photographs
Yet the images still evoke a stirring
In the consciousness
Awakening to divine beauty
Me seeking the truth and source of beauty
To compare to see if she
The Diane Gail
Is the same Goddess body beautiful
I remember memorizing years ago
And I do believe in déjà vu
Indicating being right time right place
In all creation
8-01-13

By Nolan Luke, (Narendar Puri)Naga Baba

THE GODDESS GOES FOR HER EVENING BATH

The sun has set it is 7:47 p.m.
The Goddess goes for her evening bath
So I head to my spot
Where I can see her shower

I thank Divine Mother
My vantage point
And her Grace allowing me this view
Of beauty rarely seen
Except in the visions of Saints
And the dreams of devoted Holy Men
And that includes me
I have seen the face and body
Of the Triple Goddess years ago
I have seen her smile
I have seen her with her hair wet
Unadorned she is naked truth
The Formless ISNESS behind everything
Is for a flash instant seen
In feminine embodiment
Physical glory
Spiritual grace

The Goddess
Reached down and picked up a luffa
She rubs her body

So if a cactus can be made to be soft to her skin
Then perhaps my fingers can be softer still
To touch with love and consciousness
The form seen in the real and in dreams
Watching her classic style of elegance in motion
8-01-13

By Nolan Luke, (Narendar Puri)Naga Baba

A beautiful woman taking a bath
Is a restricted sight

Here no rich attire no makeup
No colors paints or shadows or highlights
Glamor is all washed downstream
No jewels no gems
No time seen in her age
No reference
Except
The timelessness

I was stopped in my tracks
Time stood still
Time flew so fast
I blink
She is still showering
Has it now been just ten minutes
Or has it been several hours already
I cannot tell

I contemplate her bathing
In a downpour of spirit falling like rain
Drenching Creation in love unconditional
Drowning everyone in Mercy and Charity
Everyone a gazillionaire rich and wealthy

Oh that sounds like eternity
I see where and how
Just seeing the Goddess here
Without pomp without ceremony

Does send me soaring into planes beyond her form
    and being
So you begin to see why I love her so much
8-01-13

By Nolan Luke, (Narendar Puri)Naga Baba

I have become acquainted
With the scent and fragrance
Of her body perfume
The Goddess has a fragrance
My heart recognizes
Love has a specific vibration

Love has a living frequency
It has fragrance
It has color
It has tone so sweet
Heard in a voice
Seen in the color displays of courtship and mating
Inhaled and smelled in the wanton perfumes
Of deep flower blossoms beckoning come to me
In the scent beneath the perfume
Felt in the vibe between the eyes first meeting

There was a distinct subtle scent
I occasionally did detect
In the Inner Sanctum
Of the Goddess Mokambika Temple
Kullor India
In her shire room
Where she sits
Alive and awake
Astounding beauty
Strong fierce fortitude
The scent of her body comes to me
And I drift back across lifetimes

For a second I caught her timeless fragrance
8-01-13

By Nolan Luke, (Narendar Puri)Naga Baba

God must be with me
I saw her knee this morning
I see the Goddess
Her face and only a few of her features
I experience her presence
But I as yet have not seen her

Is this Goddess I see
The same as the ancient Goddess
I saw carved on old Delhi ruins
I need to see her legs
I need to know
Does this living Goddess
Have that classic Goddess derriere
I saw so well chiseled
On those surviving temple walls

An engineer without a straight line
And a poet without a clear vision
Are both apt to not follow true form
Both can miss the mark

As with the seers and poets of olden times
I have a thousand lines to write
Describing the details of her body
Before I get to describe her light
Please Goddess let me see
You in your manifest beauty
I am working here with just pen paper and ink
8-03-13

I was in contemplation
When the Goddess told me
She would be taking her shower
In five minutes

I hurried down to the river and falls
I waited
I could see her
And the two attendants
She looked my way and smiled
But as if they knew I was there
The attendants held up towels as she disrobed
And entered the waterfall

I cannot see through the waterfall
Though water be clear
She is truth
And the truth is ever veiled

So how can I verse
Those hot steamy lines of love poets
Of ancient southern India
When I need inspiration
I need to witness her features
To compose the metaphors of lushness
Sweetness and heady fragrances
That make a poet turn to hyperbole

By Nolan Luke, (Narendar Puri)Naga Baba

Just to describe
The feelings and thoughts
That truthful beauty inspires
Yes yes
I can describe her eyes
Line by line for pages and pages
Describe to you her beautiful face
I can
It changes you know
Moment to moment
Feeling to thought
She experiencing life
The world can show upon her face
The concerns of the Divine Mother
And the beauty of the Goddess
Along with the inherited material beauty
A mixture of karma fate and divine will
Beauty a Goddess could wear
And on and on it could go on and on
Poets like those old long ago Romantic mystic souls
Many in southern India
Focused their attention upon their subject matter
Love poetry of some woman seen
Evoking some Goddess form to sponsor the poem
The keeping of the meter a spun refrain
No poet works alone who writes
The grace of her presence touches as does the Muse
It is the unseen light within her that inspires

I am heading to my viewing place
A place I can peek out from behind leaves of the fig trees
And see the Goddess in her morning shower

Ah here she comes
Alone
Carrying her own towel and bags

She sits on a rock and disrobes
She steps stretches and steps into the rainbow arching waterfall
Sacred waters these become
Spirit now bathing in the spiritual light sound current
Cascading down out of eternity
The sacred becomes all the physical materiality
Spirit enlivening the elements of nature

The Goddess is manifest and real
Though she is unseen consistently
Concealed
By clear water flowing
She is within nature all nature
Behind a thin film of water
And within my heart
I have no clue or idea how or when she got there
I can only hope
The penalty for watching the Goddess bathe
Be not too severe
As I will be back later today and tomorrow

By Nolan Luke, (Narendar Puri)Naga Baba

8-04-13

THE FORMLESS ISNESS WITHIN THE GODDESS

The Formless ISNESS
Origin of Creation
Is ever unseen
Yet I see IT in everything
Especially its pure energy forms
As manifest God and Goddess
Aspects of aspects of aspects of the Formless Origin
    Source
Yet manifest identities
Each is power energy light wisdom in a particular
    individual vibration
Each on its own Plane of existence
And all Planes below

So when I glimpse the Goddess
Past the awe of her beauty
I can intuit the ISNESS within her
Truth though unseen is revealed in intuitive flashes
And as quickly I forgot
So overcome by the uplift of her beauty
I dangle above my shoes suspended
Ungrounded I smile I drift away on breezes
Feelings carry me on scented winds of remembrances
To a retreat in some Bhakti high Heaven
Clearly in the high love regions of the upper Astral
    Plane

By Nolan Luke, (Narendar Puri)Naga Baba

Ah of course the love poets artists and lovers live here
Love is the most power efficient energy in creation use it
All who dwell here
Love God personally maybe even intimately
So a reflection I see of me everywhere
Caught in God's formless embrace
Holding me aloft
Up out of matter

THE GODDESS WAS WORSHIPPED LONG BEFORE GOD WAS WORSHIPPED

Shiva is the oldest God on earth continually worshipped
His body represents divine knowledge
He often seen dancing upon the Demon of Ignorance

Shiva has four arms and four hands
One hand holds a musical device
That he clicks and taps out a rhythm we call time
In the opposite hand he holds a flame
Waving in a Puja ceremony
Burning away the Maya the illusion the veil of time
Thus opening the mind to the knowledge of eternity

Shiva is a whirling flow of time and timelessness
As Shiva is becoming manifest in creation
Both his death and rebirth are occurring simultaneously
Shiva is creator creation preserver and destroyer
Shiva is the start of activity motion and change

Shiva dances until the end of the world
Eventually we too realize
Like Shiva we must dance change in motion and activity

By Nolan Luke, (Narendar Puri)Naga Baba

While we like Shiva receive accumulate and transmit
Spiritual light and sound as energy
Shiva when he is looked upon or meditated upon
He does then to the Tenth Power transmit or broadcast
The energy in the prayer or praise
With the accumulated whirling spiritual energy within him
Back to she or he who looked upon Shiva with love in worship

8-04-13

THE GODDESS IN HER NAKED FORM

When I see the Goddess in her naked form
I get Darshan
From her eyes
As I look upon her body
Naked is her true form
As she first manifested here into existence
Perfection
The ultimate form of feminine truth and beauty
The Goddess naked
Unadorned with materiality
Unadorned with any fabric of material matter
She is truth clearly seen
She is truth with all her beauty revealed
She be truth as seen by God the Sat Nam Sohang and
    Shiva
Also my experience
And might the Formless One
Be seeing this beautiful Goddess a divine image
By looking through my eyes
For I can see
How even the Creator
Would be pleased by the beauty
Of the Goddess naked
Her spiritual light shining like a lighthouse lamp lit
Casting away all shadows of the Kali Yuga dark age

By Nolan Luke, (Narendar Puri)Naga Baba

Shining that bright light into the dark deep places
The Goddess naked lights up my day
And for the time it takes her to shower
The physical material world is so much brighter in
    light
8-05-13

I DREAMED I HELD THE GODDESS

As if I dreamed I held the Goddess last night
I remember all completely
The softness of her breath on my cheek
The tenderness of her fingers grasping me in her sleep
I could not tell at times if her body
Be asleep or awake

So close was I in her embrace
I felt her heartbeat in my chest
Each time I felt or thought my love
I could feel the cells in her body respond

The body of the Goddess
Is attune to spiritual vibrations
As real as a touch
Sensitivity akin to more subtle spiritual bodies
As if all the material spiritual body sheaths are at onement
And all spirit is transmitted into the physical
As if each sister cell in the body
Is the Goddess on the cellular level of consciousness existence
What I feel her body hears
What I think her body feels
I can hear her body thinking

By Nolan Luke, (Narendar Puri)Naga Baba

I can tell when her body is feeling secure protected
Held in my embrace
Her body has then no distractions
Her body is new again
Here is the material body of a spiritual being
The Goddess
Here on earth

Yes I am convinced that the Goddess
Has a material physical body
The Goddess has a belly button
And that says she was born of woman

This is just like in ancient long eons ago
The Goddess was born into a regular family
Was then found by a Temple
And raised to be the living Goddess of her time
So it has happened again and again all around the world

The Goddess is immaterial spirit
The Goddess is material physical
Her material body consciousness is the Goddess

Higher consciousness touches her body
Positive spirit
True love
Brings and gives peace to her body
Peace and motion
Infuses the Goddess into her body
Her body is the form
Her body is the Goddess
To be seen
To be heard
To be fully brought forth into this reality
The essence the true form and the physical body of the Goddess
More real than the dream I had of her last night
8-06-13

By Nolan Luke, (Narendar Puri)Naga Baba

THE GODDESS STEPS INTO VIEW

I see the Goddess more sweetly now
I can find no fault in the trick floor
With the sudden trap door

I fell into love
She is immaterial in esoteric energy this world experience
Yet she steps into view and can be seen
Here in this world
I am almost certain
She is material
Though I have no definite proof of the fact
I say Hello anyway
Our reality or some other
Such beauty such grace
The features of her face
Classic Goddess aspects
To describe her more I cannot
Sadly I cannot reveal any more description I do not know
Though I have seen form become invisible in eternity
While full existence and consciousness goes on
I have not yet seen her full body
I have no known body form in mind
But she could be as rumor tells it
Endowed with the Ideal Classic Dancer's body

Often carved on both facing walls leading into a shrine
And on the walls facing the inner sanctum
I observe that the material face is the Goddess on the golden face mask
That covers the Lingam Stone

By Nolan Luke, (Narendar Puri)Naga Baba

THE GODDESS BODY FORM

I was near gasping for air
Upon hearing that the Goddess
Is all curves
She has these lovely full breasts
Legs thighs hips and derriere

I listened calmly
But my heart started racing
And I fell behind in my breathing

My imagination took over
The Goddess Mookambika
In a Temple dancer's body
Those strong curvaceous calves
Sensuous smooth thighs
Gorgeous beautiful
Hips and derriere

That is the body of the Goddess
I saw in vision

The personal incarnation of the Goddess
Has that classic dancer's body
I have bitten my lip again

How can I say anything
She is shy
The Goddess a woman forever in her youth

By Nolan Luke, (Narendar Puri)Naga Baba

THE GODDESS GAVE BIRTH TO SHIVA

For some souls in feminine form
This physical incarnation as a woman
Is of the true Goddess Shakti energy
Maybe even with the Shodasi Kali aspect appearing
Though I recognized the Goddess Mookambika form
Right from the first
Yet I see the Shodasi Kali form has come into being slowly
Materializing infusing into matter
Relative reality
As it is her time
And it is her creation
Divine Mother
Is the manifest form
Of the Formless

Divine Mother
Runs the show of physical manifestation behind the scenes
So when you hear her speak
Listen attentively

Take my simple advice
Do not argue with the Goddess
Say little

Agree and do what she says
She will get her way
She owns Time
She gave birth to Creation
Yes yes yes Shiva made the creation out of himself
But Divine Mother the Goddess gave birth to Shiva

By Nolan Luke, (Narendar Puri)Naga Baba

Shiva put the process of life into the manifest creation
Soul is brought into life through birth
A life clicked in time to music
Waving the Puja flame of truth burning away the haze of time

In a short lifetime of a hundred years
We have barely time to see recognize and Self Realize
And maybe attain God Realization
All before death suddenly appears
And whisks us out of physical incarnation momentarily

The gift of the Divine Mother
Simply getting a lifetime on beautiful earth is a blessing to soul

So be very respectful
Give love
Open your heart
Anytime you are in her presence

Love
That you may receive

Air like love must be recycled
Love is like breathing

Love the Divine in any form or without a form
Know that the Divinity loves you back

Ten times your output
Be thankful be appreciative be grateful
So if she be manifesting before you
Surrender on the spot
Inquire how you may be of service to her
To me she said Love Me
So I love her in the form she appears

By Nolan Luke, (Narendar Puri)Naga Baba

THE GODDESS IN HER SHRINE

It must have been one of those fancy floor contraptions
I stood humbly before the Goddess in her shrine
I bowed reverently before her
My forehead on the ground
Maybe I lost track of time
Maybe I got a little dizzy
I stood up and looked upon her again
The floor gave way
It must have opened
Because before I knew it
I had fallen deeply in love with the Goddess
Mookambika
She of the Three Maha aspects
She is all three together as one
Singular unification of spirit
Three aspects
I have no ego in this matter above matter
I surrender

I will not even bring up the rigged floor
With its hinges lever and clasp hook
I express no complaint
That I never had a chance
I do not even know for sure if I had a choice
I saw her

More than any woman
She becomes only a few women alive at any time

By Nolan Luke, (Narendar Puri)Naga Baba

The Goddess must have seen me coming
For a long distance afar
She met me many times
Before I met her in her Shrine

Slippery floors
Then the floor was no longer there
I fell
I splashed into a giant pool of water
No not water on earth
As I easily breathe this into my very being
This water floats me
I tense and I sink
I do not drown
I relax I smile
I rise to the surface
The air is rarified
Fragrant as Heaven
The quiet of deep space
Between far distant galaxies
Aum fills the space
Om opens the door inside
The only way out of the pool
Beneath the shrine of Goddess Mookambika
So much at peace am I
Swimming floating treading water
Pitch black infinity

This underground pool is limited
But so vast
My shouts and chants and Japas
Echo forever and ever it seems
And still hear it echoing on farther
In the still further distance
I dove down I could find no bottom
The ceiling the underpinnings for the above floor
Was just maybe six feet above the water
Based on the time to fall and splash
The light illuminating the cavernous grotto
And the crystal clear water
Until the weight fell and the floor hinges
Started to close until no more light shone
Only the sound of water and air
The mind sought to leave
But the body the emotions the memories the thoughts
The inspirations those aspects of me wanted to stay
So here I am still
I have no idea how long I have been here
But I have figured out a mystery
That was only a mystery because
It was obvious
Beneath the trick floors
Of Mookambika Shrine and Temple
Lies what must be an underground aquafer
Of water energized by the Love of the Goddess

By Nolan Luke, (Narendar Puri)Naga Baba

Showering down on those before her
So the floors in addition to being rigged
Are pervious to the love she bestows
So maybe this might even be
Her love and her tears shed
Listening intently to the heart
While the plea and wish and prayer are heard
Though she slew a giant Demon with a trident
Her heart is the compassion of the birth mother
Shiva may have created the creation
But when the creation is threatened
Whose fierce killing sword protects and defends
who attacks battles and eliminates the threat
Mother Divine Mother
An army in her heart she never tires she fights
Yet her love suspends us even when we disbelieve
Even when we doubt her will and existence
She loves and believes in this creation and us
As if she knows something we don't
I am sure she knows where I am
I don't
I have come to believe I float in a pool
Of the tears of the Goddess
Shed over these many centuries
With all the love blessings well wishes fulfilled
This is some of the purest water south of eternity
This is Love in a liquid medium

I would not expect love to be a solid
Love is never rigid enough to stay one shape and size
Long enough to be considered a solid form

Love is a liquid we can easily breathe
Love is a nutrient to the spirit as is truth
Love is the womb of the Divine Mother

First there is the Creation
And then Divine Mother comes along
And puts life within the creation
Within everything
Within every being
Within every body
Within every cell

According to the story
Creation got built by the hands of Shiva
The Goddess furnished the three worlds and carried
    the water
She had the household chores duties and labors of the
    world to do
She is mother to the planet and the heavens
Divine Mother has been watching over creation
A whole lot longer than this manifested existence
Like a great Mother she wants her children to go on
    and beyond
Her love is the magic salve that soothes
Her understanding comforts
Her Darshan enlivens us

By Nolan Luke, (Narendar Puri)Naga Baba

Surely I can rally enough of me to get out of here
Me in a deep pool of love
No steps no ladder

Deep in love
Some might say
But then I have been deep in love with God before
Almost everyone has
Especially when we were little children
God was real
Because we could easily feel the truth

The part of me I kept close to my making
I kept God to myself
I shared little with only a few
Personal and intimate
It remains a one on one
Even though the one is seen as many
All is true
Everyone is correct
Everyone is every on the path to God
We just have to move in Its direction

So unexpected the Goddess early
Did appear to me this lifetime
I nearly forgot
So long ago it has been
So I float here content
Trapped in the love of the Goddess
I may have been tricked into falling
Deep in love with the Goddess
Which reminds me

By Nolan Luke, (Narendar Puri)Naga Baba

Might it be time the evening bath
Of the Goddess be happening now
Somehow
I am still on the floor my forehead still touches stone
I very slowly get a foot under me
And not too steady I get my legs
I stand and view the divine golden image
I saw the unseen she gave me a side glance smile
It sparkled on the air
As if the molecules were tinkling
I walked away following the queue
To outside the temple
The bright sun overhead
Pilgrims Priest and Holy Men filled the courtyard
I blinked adjusting to the light
We walked out the temple
I found my shoes
Right where I left them
Out in the open in the sun
Except my shoes were wet inside
I slushed and squeaked
Unable to tell why or how my shoes were wet inside
Sometimes the mysteries are obvious
Sometimes the mysteries defy explanation
I could only wonder
Where begin and end mystery miracles and wishes
Limited by time
Yet enough room to now and then squeeze in eternity
8-05-13

THE GODDESS IN YOUR EYES

Oh let me see the Goddess in your eyes
I see her when you stare or gaze
Let me see the Goddess
that I may look upon her
I want to contemplate her beauty
She the truth I see and experience
I am better than any mirror
Magic or otherwise
A mirror reflects image back reversed
I see the surface and beneath the outer sometimes
I sometimes see the Inner
And sometimes a step or two beyond
I can express the feelings your poses provoke
In me and nearly all men
We are pre wired for Beauty
You turn heads
So many Goddesses you have been
True beauty seen in a side glance
From every angle you are beautiful
Feminine beauty and grace
Personified
Beautiful symmetry
Buttocks firm round curves
From every view a beauty
Her legs a marvel of nature to see
The curve of her breast so pretty

By Nolan Luke, (Narendar Puri)Naga Baba

Real beauty holding the light of the Goddess
In you
8-08-13

So much advice and scholarship
On the subject of love and union
Written in the long ago past
And updated and repeated in the present
Will not improve the future

Written mainly by men
The errors are outrageous
To us today

But somehow to this day
Men believe a myth made by men
About women who they feared and did not understand
Or hated jealousy and envy
To such an extent
Most ancient so called wise men dehumanized woman
Devalued her true worth
And then proceeded to brainwash her into not thinking

People say it is the custom
Some say God made it so
An outrage repeated a thousand times
Is still an outrage

Besides
We exist in Duality
Anyone who believes that dribble of women being evil

Suffers that fate of accepting that the feminine yin nature
Balancing their masculine yang nature is evil
Therefore man is corrupt because half of himself is evil
That line of thinking does not lead to freedom liberation or God
Do not judge what you do not understand
8-08-13

CHAPTER THREE

THE CREATOR

By Nolan Luke, (Narendar Puri)Naga Baba

BEAUTY PERSONIFIED

I ran out of paper
Not a blank sheet to be found anywhere
Then
Diane directed me to a box of her old things
I found this journal of hers from years ago
I think she moved back in with me
Where earlier today I had the impulse to call her
On the telephone
I felt her that close
I bumped into her this afternoon
The air takes on a peaceful grace
When she is present
Sounds have musical qualities
I smile for no reason
That can be seen
I hum little tunes I do not know
Red orange is the sunset
About the time I would see her face on her way home
Beautiful
She sees me and smiles
Her face her smile so fresh
As if the first sight and smile
All over again
For the first time again
The leap the heart takes
Uplifting Soul out of body
The effect of seeing the divine light
In the form of beauty personified

The image of the woman the Goddess
All in a glance
9-06-13

By Nolan Luke, (Narendar Puri)Naga Baba

THE CREATOR   I

How much does the Creator love us
We conscious aware beings
We are the point of creation
We are the result of creation
We be the product and reward of creation
Creation is the process
Creation is the means
To bring about the illumination of Atman Soul
Consciousness
That Soul see recognize itself as the true identity

The Creation leads back to the Sugmad Vortex
The whirlpool of light sound surrounding
The fountain of Spirit manifesting out of the
Nothingness center
Soul drops its perfect true form on the Soul Plane
Becoming invisible on the Alak Plane
Becoming Formless Spirit consciousness
As Formless Spirit see hear experience
And realize God Creator as the Origin Source
The conscious Supreme Being
The Absolute
The Beginning
The Singularity
Ever manifesting into existence
Out of Nothingness

Out of Voidness
Ever unmanifest
Yet unseen unheard
Hidden by the Nothingness
The Creator is unknown
In ITS unmanifestness

By Nolan Luke, (Narendar Puri)Naga Baba

THE CREATOR II

Unmanifest
The Creator is beyond our Creation matrix
Our conscious awareness
Stops at the Nothingness center
I know
For I have stared forever at the Nothingness Center
Nothingness
Void
Nothing
Not a thing
Bam flash
Sound light
Thunder beam
Word bright
Shining spirit
Bright with fire
Spirit light and sound
Unlimited power pouring forth
Looking deep into the fountain of spirit light
Deep within the Nothingness
There is glow at the base of the shining light
Goodness
Goodness in ITS unmanifest aspect
Goodness beyond our spiritual comprehension
Goodness beyond greatness and superiority
Unmanifest

Not yet apparent
Yet it is here now
Hear the word of light spoken out of Nothingness
9-07-13

By Nolan Luke, (Narendar Puri)Naga Baba

III

Creation is reflected and seen in a woman's body
The Manifestation is feminine
Woman reflects the Creation
The Creation reflects the Unseen Unheard

The beauty of a woman seen and heard
Is a salve for the wounds of battle
Sends artists of all kinds to their media
Is Soul's first glimpse of divinity

The truth beauty grace of a woman
Reveals the temple that the Goddess dwells within
As well as manifests the power of creativity
Arousing the passions of artist expression for all to
    see

The Goddess inspires
She encourages the arts
The Goddess disguises as the Muse
She draws intuition into art form

Art can affect the observer
Art can lift the consciousness
Art can give us insight into ourselves and others
Art can liberate the spirit free

The Goddess blesses the arts with creative energy

Because art enlivens the spirit within
Stirs the conscious attention
Inward and outward simultaneously
Revealing we truly be formless spirit manifesting in material form
Surrounded by the beauty in art and nature
The timeless moments
Representing the creative moment of art out of inspiration
Seen in art experienced

The Goddess bestows her blessings raining down upon us all
Love Beauty Joy and her divine grace
9-07-13

By Nolan Luke, (Narendar Puri)Naga Baba

IV

We must be precious to the Creator
IT must love us
More than we can imagine
If IT stops refreshing Creation
All falls down
If IT stops loving us
We whittle back to nothingness
IT gives of ITSELF
To crank all this into manifestation
Sacrifice
IT mothers the Creation into existence
And then sets the Creation on its own
Spins everything into a flowing stream
With love humor and mercy ITS attributes
IT remains behind the scenes unseen
As the stage play starring every one of us goes on
The title of the stage play
"Consciousness"
The maturation of formless spirit
Like any good plot maker
The Creator stirred in freewill and choice
Permitting the characters to make up their own lives
Allowing the characters to decide for themselves
How to play themselves
And how to act
This kind of production takes patience and humor
Creation is not a business with a profit to the Maker

Creation is a gift shared
Between Creator and the Created
9-07-13

By Nolan Luke, (Narendar Puri)Naga Baba

SIREN CALL

Back before the time
That women's minds were turned inside out
Scrubbed scraped and thoroughly soundly beaten
Along with a thorough washing of the brain
Then the men funneled into ears and brain
The ridiculous myth
That substantiates the enslavement of the female to
    the male

Wake up Girl
Wake up Soul
Wake up Spirit

You've been conned swindled deceived enslaved
Into believing that which is not in your own best
    interest

You may have been fed a poison pill
Guilt
Upon you and your gender
Where is there any evidence of guilt
Where is there evidence of any crime
What are the particulars

Prison is believing and living a lie
The bars fences and locks work
Because you agree to believe

So long as you agree
You cannot complain about the harsh treatment
9-02-13

By Nolan Luke, (Narendar Puri)Naga Baba

SHE TOUCHED ME

My love reached across the space
And touched me on my hand
As soft as a moth landing on my fingers
Her magnetic sensuality I feel
That scent her fragrance
Triggered a hundred memories
Brain overload
All I can see is her
Filling the vision of the divine image
I lose gravity to the ground
My toes no longer reach the floor
I slide out of my shoes
I sniff the perfume behind her ear
I soar up through the ceiling the roof the sky
She takes a grip on me
And somehow carries me away
Now she is teasing me with her fingers
Fluttering almost touching my face chest arms
I feel the vibrations of her emotions
Even in silence I hear her voice whispering
She loves me
As if I could forget
I am always reminded
When I shout out
I love you Diane Gail
As if speaking to empty air

Yet she wraps her arms around my shoulder
Leans in and gives me a kiss
On my forehead cheek neck twice kissed

By Nolan Luke, (Narendar Puri)Naga Baba

A DIRECT CALL FROM SACH KHAND

Always a good girl
No matter how sexy she be
Always a good girl
Even when she got a little naughty

Always the Goddess
Even when she was as salty as a sailor
Always the Goddess
Even while attaining Jivan Mukti

Diane Gail
Came into this world
Lived her life very well as Soul
She left self realized

She placed a direct call from Sach Khand
The next day
That I not worry
She arrived home safely

She was one of the prettiest girls I ever met
She still makes me catch my breath
Whenever I happen to see her
Or an image of her as in a quick glance

I see her in my peripheral vision
She commutes from Eternity
Visits stays for a while and travels distances
Always always a good dear friend
9-07-13

By Nolan Luke, (Narendar Puri)Naga Baba

THE ISNESS

What is Unmanifest
What was preexistent
What was not yet here

What existed unmanifested prior to manifestation
Into existence

The ISNESS is the all unseen unheard
The ISNESS is SOUND LIGHT SOUND LIGHT SOUND LIGHT SOUND LIGHT....
The ISNESS without form or kind name or like
The ISNESS intersects the beginning point of Creation
And the center point of Nothingness
And the end point of Soul's long journey back home as conscious formless Spirit

The ISNESS spoke
And the worlds began
ISNESS repeatedly speaks that word
The Sound Light word that is Spirit
The Streaming Life Current of spiritual energy
Filling the expansiveness of the ever manifesting Creation the first rain and flood
Filling the surrounding Nothingness
With the vastness of eternity
And topping eternity with infinity beyond

These eternal rivers and streams eventually flow downstream

By Nolan Luke, (Narendar Puri)Naga Baba

Cascading down as rain as waterfalls
As mist as showers
New created Spirits
Be the oxygen pumped into an aquarium
As well as the nutrients
For all living beings everywhere in existence
Down through the levels of existence
Down through the Twelve Planes of existence
Down across and cascading Shiva's dreadlocks
    flowing
Down into the earth's sacred waters
Spirit rains down on earth
Spirit appears as sunlight
Spirit is heard in the sounds of nature and humans
Spirit is seen in everything living and inert
Spirit is the composite single center dark hollow
Of a solar sun
All solar suns die
Their burnt out ash soot dust particle remains
Make up a content of our chemical structure
All of Creation am I and you
Everything that has happened in the past is me
The past is recycled in me
Consciousness in the moment
All of me is living now in this moment
Here
Far flung particles from all over the universe
Be the scoop of clay and scoop of water
That make up my material form
All at onement is unity given life within me

THE SPIRITUAL TRAVELLER'S GUIDEBOOK TO ETERNITY

By Nolan Luke, (Narendar Puri)Naga Baba

A galaxy exists within each of us
Worlds that live independent from us
Systems tissues organs
Each with a separate language
And biometric structure
Levels upon levels of operation
Motor mechanical
Hyperbaric pressurized systems
Foreign suppression and identification squads
Of one's own immune system
Running best when
One's self identity is clear at peace at center of beingness
A healthy self identity is being honest with one's self
Forgive yourself accept yourself
Appreciate the different aspects of self
Unify all aspects of the self
Into a single image of self
Be thankful for everything
Unilaterally forgive everyone
Unilaterally take one hundred percent of the blame for everything
Having taken full responsibility
You now have full authority to change the situation
By changing yourself
Change into your true self
Help bring order harmony balance to the cosmos
By doing so within
Do your part to be a good citizen of the cosmos
Travel the worlds within or the worlds beyond ourselves

Generate light
Be a light within and to others
9-08-13

By Nolan Luke, (Narendar Puri)Naga Baba

THE TRUE REFLECTION OF FORMLESS SPIRIT

The true reflection of formless spirit
And the true form of self as Soul Consciousness
Both the same Oneness
Be made directly out of the supreme divine image
The Formless ISNESS
The Consciousness that begat Creation
Truth Light and Sound
Reflect down from the Origin Source
Truth Light and Sound
Reflect within us
Truth Light and Sound
Reflect back to the Creator

A closer divine image to view and reflect
Might be the Goddess or God
Might be a Guru
Seen within

With spiritual help or on one's own
We choose with our freewill
ISNESS be the Nothingness center in everything
We are able to reflect back
To the Guru the Goddess the God in our life
When we choose to act or not to act
Reflecting the light is the correct choice and action
Someone near you might benefit from the light
Working for Goddess or God has never been easier
9-08-13

THE UNMANIFEST ISNESS

The unmanifest ISNESS
Divine energy
Though to us unmanifest
Seems to be before the Creation event

We do not meet the Reality that is Unmanifest
IT at some point
Prior to manifesting ITSELF
Into a dimension other than ITSELF
Into a Nothingness Void
IT is separate from us
IT keeps us separate
We the Creation be ITS other

ISNESS may hold all potential existence
Yet ISNESS by ITSELF
Is being by ITSELF
In ITS Unmanifest existence
Divine Intelligence
The one Singularity
May have understood ITS ALLNESS
The realization of being alone
The experience of aloneness
Can Unmanifest ISNESS know loneliness
Can the pre manifest know love
Yes in the capacity of ISNESS
Perhaps love came as a result of manifestation

By Nolan Luke, (Narendar Puri)Naga Baba

The Unmanifest is GOODNESS pure and true
The Manifest Creation is ITS consort

Oh the Secrets of the Sugmad
I could tell
But that would simply be jumping ahead
Of the story told

Something about this manifestation of us
Appeals to the Unmanifest Origin Source
IT loves us true
Yet IT wants to play with us
IT enjoys touching us individually
IT can kiss us through other people and beings
IT loves a good story
IT opens to a true love story
IT appreciates a good joke told well in real time
IT has a sweet tooth formless without
Love unconditional to Goddess or God
Is a candy morsel
The Creator is so easily smitten
IT sends back ten times the power love
In addition to love from Goddess and or God

Soul you need to understand the Formless
Creation is not a break even proposition
Something unlimited has to supply Creation
Something unknown must be that something for this
Something unmanifest experiences the love given to
    IT
The Formless Isness of light and sound manifestation

When we love Goddess or God IT feels the love

By Nolan Luke, (Narendar Puri)Naga Baba

All love made contributes to the cosmic wave flow

Lovemaking is the cosmic principle personified
Lovemaking is an ultimate absolute means to Goddess and God
Lovemaking is a sacred tantra vehicle to the absolute Supreme
9-8-13

CHAPTER FOUR

THE UNIVERSAL BELOVED

By Nolan Luke, (Narendar Puri)Naga Baba

MY BELOVED SAID

My Beloved said to me
Nolan
Your etheric body intuition hears me clear and true
Your intuition sees me clear and true
It is the mind that stumbles in on our meetings
In this brief bright illumination of timelessness
The intuitive flash seen in these Etheric skies
In between the Par Brahm and the Void above
Out of that fine sparkly fabric I cover myself
Visible to you
And within your reach
So sweet love embrace my light
Kiss my lips
Close your eyes
See me clear and true to life
Hold me tight
Tell me again
What did we last say
Oh yes
We had just said
I love you
Just before I let the body go
I Soul made the choice to leave when I did
And you caught the understanding humor
Of leaving while you were not looking
All in an intuitive instant above time space and matter

By Nolan Luke, (Narendar Puri)Naga Baba

Here in almost eternal timelessness
Very little time permeates this Etheric region
While light from Sat Loka above brightens it so
The Etheric reflects the Soul plane far above it
Like a bright shadow out of light matter
Reflecting the form of the Soul light body
The etheric material is airy and shiny bright
In the etheric body on the Etheric plane
Everything is as real
As things are real to you on earth
Things exist here
Worlds rarely described
Heavily populated areas
And vast open landscapes stretching forever it seems
And not a Soul to be found
Out here in the upper vastness
We meet above shadows and night
A heaven so slow is the time
That a nice embrace hug and kiss
Can easily last a week of earth time
Yet the entire Etheric experience
That quick fast flash
Is the speed of a camera shutter click
Open close
Everything seen in a quick brief moment
Even the impression we embraced
Here on the Etheric plane turning so so slow
This my Beloved said to me
Just a moment ago
6-22-13

I LOOKED AT BEAUTY

I know we mortals are not supposed to watch
Goddesses when they bathe
Especially in sacred waters

The penalty I know
Is to be forever moved and affected by beauty and truth

And so it was one mid afternoon
I had chanced upon a field of wildflowers
Well off the path I was on that wound through the forest
My God there she was
I knew not her name
Or who worships her
Or what may be their rites and rituals
But there she was dancing
Naked in daylight
Her feminine form was a true vision
And her Shakti magnetic wave energy
Encoiled
Grabbed me
Held me
Captured me
The spell of true beauty vibrating radiating an image
Even a blind man can see
With my physical eyes I see before me

By Nolan Luke, (Narendar Puri)Naga Baba

A stunning woman so material so sensual
Yet I see the invisible light of her
Beauty I thus experience just as does any Yogi with
    eyes closed
She touches me and I am beyond myself into bliss

Her dance took me from physical
To some place deep within
Yet far far up there somewhere near the Tisra Til
Above the matrix of time
I see her timelessly
Ageless she seems
Moving like air like water
Through ether and over earth
I lost time somewhere near dusk
She danced until dark

I finally took a breath
I inhaled
I must have forgotten to breathe all afternoon
I was parched
And my canteen was empty
So down to the river I went quietly
And there she was in the water bathing
There I was mesmerized again
I forgot to fill my canteen
My shoes had filled with water
I watched her from behind a think patch of cattails
The dusks of evening descending
Went past the purple in the dim the dark and the shadows
Suddenly into night
The moon rising on the horizon hill
My eyes adjusted to the moonlight
But she was gone
From view

By Nolan Luke, (Narendar Puri)Naga Baba

I filled my canteen and headed back to the path
I had left earlier in the day to get water for my canteen
6-25-13

I SHOULD NOT WRITE DOWN

My Beloved said to me
She said
I am living in happiness
But I wish I could cry a tear
My Beloved said
I have everything in creation
But I don't have you here
In eternity with me
God is everything
God made you and me
We love each other so well because we love God first
I Soul Diane Gail may be anywhere
And always have my heart filled with love
Direct from the Source the Creator light sound Vortex and spirit fountain
The overflow love we extend to others as good will charity
God gives us the means to love unconditionally
As IT so loves us

My Beloved said
So for us to love each other
Is to love the creation
Is to love the Creator
For ITS spark ignited imagination into conception manifesting a formless formation
Of Spirit light sound as current
Out of unmanifest Nothingness
At the center the source of everything
Made in ITS formless image

By Nolan Luke, (Narendar Puri)Naga Baba

Love is the celebration of existence
Embracing us
In the spiral soaring up
On wings of light
Becoming at onement with sound and the everything
So meet me in your dreams
Hold me tight
Kiss me sweet
And tell me you love me
All this is what my Beloved said
6-25-13

THAT FORMLESS SINGULARITY

My Beloved is
THE BELOVED
That so many poets mystics saints holy men and yoginis speak about
The oneness
The Isness
That formless singularity
A paradox contradiction abstractness
Without form
Without name
Spinning spinning
A churning vortex of light and sound
Circling downward
Into nothingness
Then comes the fountain and spray
The secret shown revealed displayed

Being and Souls and other formless individualized spirit consciousness
Bear ITS impression
Kabir of Benares
Stood at the Rim
And he peeked over
He saw
He calls it the Aravamuda
And the sweet nectar it churns
Into manifest existence

By Nolan Luke, (Narendar Puri)Naga Baba

Sustains the entire creation
Keeping everything animated connected
And nourished with the light sound nectar

Kabir of Benares 15th century Bhakti Sant
My first Spiritual Traveller and guide this lifetime
He a Muslim rug weaver travelled to the Aravamuda
He drank too much too often that divine nectar spirit
    wine
And time and time again
Was he inebriated
People slandered him
Said he was drunk and crazy
He drank no alcohol
Eyes closed he said he saw the Divine
While he out loud described IT
For all to hear
Kabir could not hold his tongue still
So much under the influence was he
Of that nectar that true intoxicate ambrosia brew
It renders the ego a mute obedient servant to Soul
It dissolves the fetters that chain Soul to the material
    Earth
It uplifts the mind into peace and illumination
It uplifts Soul into eternity and beyond into infinity
It turns everything upside down in the mind
Inside outside
Great Soul Kabir
Walked the far country skies up beyond invisibility
So much of the day
Spent at his loom sitting cross legged on the floor
That he may have walked about
On legs a little wobbly at times
But then sitting there so long
Could have the same sometime stumble effect

By Nolan Luke, (Narendar Puri)Naga Baba

So no no he drank no material wine no alcohol of any kind
Kabir offended no Soul

Kabir did offend many egos
Kabir did get accused of offending everyone
Kabir spoke all his poems impromptu
He did not know how to read or write
Yet he was learned
He spoke the truth the absolute truth
He became filled with this nectar
He became filled with love joy goodness and truth
Soon he was overflowing
And his poems he shouted aloud
While sometimes pound the beat with his feet
Kabir would start singing
Which was not the problem
It was the truths he said in his singing
Which he did full voice out loud
Kabir did not stir factions one against another
Kabir stirred up things within the individual
Kabir had enemies in every faction
At times it seems
Nearly everyone at one time or another
Wanted his head removed from his body
Kabir continued to imbibe that nectar divine
It carried him far away from here
He told his travels
Described the sights he had seen
Going to and coming back from
The house of his Beloved
He tells us the door is open
Everyone is expected back home
Kabir visited every day
There too he drank too much

By Nolan Luke, (Narendar Puri)Naga Baba

Kabir of Benares
Loved the Divine so much
And to such an extent
He had to love fully
He had to attach himself to the Creator
Kabir needed to love more everyday
Because his heart expanded every night
He awoke each day
Already filled with love of God
Love in God
And being loved by God
He generated more love
In his lifelong love of his wife
He generated even more love
Loving his children
Loving all travellers on the road of spirit
Loving those who loved him
Loving especially those who declared themselves his
        enemy
And to his slanderers
He bestowed his love
And in addition
A prayer to God that they live a thousand years
Kabir could afford to be generous
Kabir was a rich man
He gave away his entire fortune every day
He died every night and went home
Kabir lived his life in love every day
Kabir the weaver the poet the Great Soul the Sant

Ever near when lovingly his name is called
Kabir appears to show the way from here to Hereness
    now
6-26-13

By Nolan Luke, (Narendar Puri)Naga Baba

WHEN I WAS A KID

When I was just a kid nine and a half to ten
God sent Kabir of Benares to me

I was confused and not sure of anything
About the world and me

Kabir reassured and taught me
About the world the worlds beyond the world and me

I learned there is a plan
Be patient be alert and wait

For everyone there is a plan
We just need to live long enough to realize it

He said do not waste this lifetime
Love and even love too much

He said I must find my living teacher guru
Even if I find God first

Kabir opened the world the Sun and the universe
Pointed out the shortcuts between planes

On travels he talked about God and the Beloved
As if they were one

Kabir instilled the love of spiritual travel
Riding that sound light wave across heavens
Beyond the inaccessible regions all the way to home
6-26-13

By Nolan Luke, (Narendar Puri)Naga Baba

When I was around eight years old
I was freaking out
I was scared that I had missed my mark
Maybe wrong planet
Wrong country wrong family wrong body

I kept waiting since after infancy
For the Robed men to come to the door
I needed to get to a temple or monastery
I needed to begin dedicating this life
I knew I was getting too old to be found
I was in despair
I lost the desire to go on
Life as an eight year old
Held no promise
Had no meaning
I wanted to leave
So one day when no one was in my Grandmother's house but me
I went into her kitchen
And chose a knife that was the sharpest
I was ready to go
I raised up the knife
And a blue skin man appeared
He stopped me
He said I was at the right place
At the right time
He said everything would be fine
And it was
6-26-13

FORMLESS SPIRIT

On our approach to the Creator
We see that God has different names
Depending on how it is seen
From where you are standing
To which Plane are you looking

Of course we are ever looking within
To see the way before us

We are never alone
We are never lost
We are always saved
When we turn within

Even in Eternity we turn within

The nothingness center within us
When our consciousness
Is formless spirit
Is the same Nothingness
As the Nothingness center
At the bottom center
Of the Aravamuda spinning

Somewhere all Nothingness does touch the unmanifest God

By Nolan Luke, (Narendar Puri)Naga Baba

We each everything is pinned tight to the manifestation grid
We cannot be lost or alone or too far away
Even the hollow pit we can sometimes feel within
Is maybe the shared dark center of the Creator
Maybe the Creator feels the pain and sorrow of separation more than you think
6-28-13

JUST BELOW THE SURFACE

My Beloved
Peered down into the lake waters
I could see the water surface there above me
Her face so fresh so young I could see her eyes
Through the murkiness of the Void
I could almost touch her
Standing on tiptoes on earth
My face now just below the water surface
My neck was straining
I pursed my lips
Her face entered the water
Our lips kissed
Again
Again
Wow
We smiled

Soul ingenuity

Origination in creation
Cause overcoming obstacles
Creativity bringing about a kiss
In the waters of the Mansarover Lake

By Nolan Luke, (Narendar Puri)Naga Baba

My Beloved she waits for me
Love ties us bound to each other
Across all divides
Freedom and liberation at work in eternity
6-29-13

JUST SIX SECONDS AWAY

My Beloved
Seized me by the ears again
A memory a melody
She dragged me off to some far flung galaxy I know
    not
Seems she was in a hurry of sorts
To get me to see a sunrise here
On a Pink Blue Green planet
Revolving around
A far away double solar sun
Brilliant
Each casting a different color light
We were just in time
Dawn awakened here
But over there see
Pink and yellow sunbeams
Lit the night and shadows brightening
This world still in its Eden cycle
Its golden age of transcendence
Spirit Soul in airy bodies
Young world young body forms
Sweetness of air
Soft earth ground
Delicate green growing everywhere
A trillion colors flashing
Flowers wings and insects buzzing

By Nolan Luke, (Narendar Puri)Naga Baba

Life in different hues
All these things we view
Watching a day rise and come into being
Sometimes unexpected
We get to be together in a faraway brand new day
6-30-13

LOVE FREEDOM AND LIBERTY

When Soul has Love Freedom and Liberty
It does not need power
Control is attachment
Fear is imprisonment

In eternity GOODNESS is power
In eternity LOVE is power
In eternity MERCY is power
In eternity SPIRIT is power

In the material existence
The abstract qualities of God
Stirred into the matter of life
Enlivens the making of a good human being

The first step to self-realization
Of self as Soul
Is becoming a good human being
A good citizen of the cosmos
A welcome visitor to shrines and temples
A witness to things unseen

The control of creation running
Is the reinforcement of more love more spirit
So dearly does love the Creator its creation
ITS keen eye and ear to each everything existing

By Nolan Luke, (Narendar Puri)Naga Baba

So soul lives love freedom and liberty
Exercising a practice of Beingness
7-01-13

THE GODDESS MOOKAMBIKA

The Goddess Mookambika
Manifested into the physical material
As the Devi Adi Shakti
The union of
Maha Kali
Maha Lakshmi
And Maha Sarasvati

The Goddess Mookambika
Appears with Shiva and Vishnu
The feminine and masculine
Are principles of one same divinity

Here is one of the greatest centers
Of Shakti worship
One of the Seven famous sacred places

Adi Sankara
Installed the Jyotirlinga
In about the eighth century AD

The Sri Mookambika temple of Kalluru India
Has been an active center
Of Shakti worship since
The tenth century AD
Though its antiquity dates back to some earlier era.

By Nolan Luke, (Narendar Puri)Naga Baba

Ade Shakti is Mookambika
The Goddess Mookambika is Adi Shakti
In the Linga form
She personifies represents embodies and exteriorizes
    manifest creation
She maintains protects and defends the creation
She extends the life of the creation
She oversees the dissolution of creation
She slays demons that threaten creation
She slayed the giant demon Mookasura
Sometimes also called the demon Kalloasura
She stood seventy miles tall and beautiful
The trident she used to kill the demon
Is still within reach
Forty-two feet tall steel trident
With not yet a speck of rust anywhere upon it
So mighty was the battle fought and won
Such an expenditure of strength and energy
She laid down to rest she slept
She rested her head on the mountains as pillows
Resting her feet in the sea
From her ankles to the inner temple in the forest
    jungle
Is approximately thirty miles
The mighty spirit that is the Goddess Mookambika
Resides in her temple
And special days of the year
She rides around her temple in a golden Cinderella
    pumpkin carriage
Pulled by priest and devotee

Warrior though she be when needed
Mookambika with her trusty trident ready
Is the benevolent Mother
The living presence of the Mother Goddess on earth

The Goddess Mookambika
She sees with three eyes
She works with four hands

Mookambika is a Goddess of victory
Mookambika is a Goddess of wishes

Kolluru temple of Mookambika
Has conducted worship ritual and ceremony
Continually for thirteen hundred years
Here the individual divine presence
Of the Divine Mother
The Mother Goddess
The great trinity of Goddesses
The three great Goddesses merged together into one
    union
The Goddess Mookambika
Her great divine presence
Is felt within the fortress thick outer walls
Her Divine presence is a personal spiritual experience
    while within the inner sanctum
Divine love slays the demon
Restoring peace and prosperity after victory and wish
    fulfilled
Touched by her living presence every time while
    standing in line

By Nolan Luke, (Narendar Puri)Naga Baba

While composing a wish to ask of her when again
 before her
The Goddess Mookambika is alive
She waits for me to return to her
To fulfill my vows to her for wishes to be granted and
 fulfilled some day
7-02-13

MENTAL FOCUS

I Soul like to stretch the mind open
And pour in as much light and sound as I can

Like getting it to focus
On that instant just prior to Creation

And tell it to Stay
Is like placing a doggie treat on the nose of a dog

Nothing equals nothing
Yet nothing holds the unimagined all

The all of everything is the One unseen
Beyond name and form

Considering Formlessness
The mind is just a puppy happily chasing its tail

Until it exhausts and flops at your feet
Tired and sleepy

Consciousness is light sound vibration
It fills the mind
Enlightens the mind
Transforms the mind
Becoming the Divine Mind

By Nolan Luke, (Narendar Puri)Naga Baba

Disciplined obedient waiting for command
The mind does as told by Soul
7-02-13

SPIRIT

Each individual spirit created out of nothingness
Starts off like an undifferentiated cell
A stem cell in the body formless

Spirit formless light is blank
Experience in creation will fill it

Freewill and choice
Fate and predestination
Cause and effect
Abstract and concrete
A few of the many lessons to learn
Coming back up the Planes

Spirit individualizes itself in form
In its true form visible
Spirit is the Soul Consciousness light
On the Sat Lok Soul Plane
And the immaterial etheric intuitive
The mental material sheath
The physical material body form

Some ancients speculated
That a human can be made in nine million years
Give or take a millennium for acquiring spiritual
    consciousness

By Nolan Luke, (Narendar Puri)Naga Baba

We become Soul Conscious Aware Human Beings
Helping the next soul up the staircase
7-03-13

THE SHABDANAM

The Shabdanam
The audible life current
The spiritual light sound stream
The true formless word issued forth
Through everything and everyone
Is heard listening within
Contact with lightsound
Generates joy happiness and excitement
Awakening Soul to conscious awareness
The sound brightens the eyes
The light tingles the ears
All is reverse alternating
Sound to light to sound
Wave to particle to wave
Direct to alternating current to direct
It changes yet is ever the same
It energizes and charges
The rest points in eternity
And the forms of materiality

The Shabdanam
Is also a return wave
Back to the true origin center of all
As the return wave current
The soundlight is called the BANI

By Nolan Luke, (Narendar Puri)Naga Baba

The BANI flows back to the beginning of everything
Ease into the current and the wind
The express route out of the material
Through the immaterial across the Void
Into visible eternity through the invisible eternity to
      Formlessness
7-04-13

THE ONE DIVINITY

The one deity
Is the one same divinity
That each and every religion worships

No one perspective
Or multiple perspectives
Or all and every perspective combined
Can grasp the allness
That is the ISNESS

Every perspective
Every possible proximity
Has a sight line
And a basic valid foundation
For their perspective

Each and every one is correct
Yet no one knows the name
Of the one deity
Yet the Nameless One has one hundred trillion names
In even the tiniest of galaxies
No one can completely describe the Formless ISNESS

Stand there before IT
And try and describe what you see and hear and
    experience
One will run out of time

By Nolan Luke, (Narendar Puri)Naga Baba

The Creator of everything is eternal
And ever the beginning
IT is beyond our finite experiences and lifetimes
IT is beyond definition and exclusivity
IT exists beyond its own manifestation into existence
IT exists Unmanifest giving only a peek inside
    Nothingness
7-05-13

WE LEARN GOD IS LOVE

The Creator gives us objects of Love
To love in order to practice the exercise of Love
We learn to love each other over lifetimes
In various body forms
And with different levels of conscious awareness

Each of us is the offspring
Of the ISNESS which loves us
We in turn love our offspring
We eventually love those souls they love
And their offspring
Thus our love grows beyond ourselves
Our spiritual goodwill extends to the world
We love the many Souls who comprise our ancestors
We experience being the object of love
We become ever the subject viewing the object
With love admiration and joy
We learn GOD while learning love
We learn GOD while learning charity and forgiveness
We learn the Self while loving another
We acquire the truth of Self in Self Realization
With help we free ourselves of all materials
Naked we return to the Creator
No coverings no form
GOD's light shines through us
Formless spirit light we be
We each exist as Consciousness Individualized

By Nolan Luke, (Narendar Puri)Naga Baba

Bhakti love to Guru
Bhakti love to GOD
Prepares us to be the love object of GOD as the subject loving
So deeply loved we drown in a sea of love and mercy

In the ocean of love and mercy
The wind is GOD's GRACE
GOD's GOODNESS nourishes all
The ocean itself is sweet nectar
Yet
It is just the overflow
See there the Sun in the sky Eternity
That is GOD the Beginning
The Lamakan Sun
Seen from afar from the ocean of love and mercy

So to the golden sun we go
Closer up
A shining mist covers the sun singing
Ah
The light is a VORTEX swirling loudly
Like the rim of a whirlpool
Downpulling
Oh it so churns
This action Kabir the weaver poet of Benares
Named and called the Aravamuda
Churning a sweet nectar fountain up out of Nothingness
Imagine looking into nothingness forever
When out of nowhere out of oblivion out of blank emptiness
Out of voidness comes a thunderous burst of spirit gushing rushing
Up falling on all as spiritual rain
From formless to form to material
And back to form to formlessness
GOD is LOVE as are we as be all   7-09-13

By Nolan Luke, (Narendar Puri)Naga Baba

ETERNITY

Soul must exercise patience
Here and Now
As eternity is timeless

Time denotes beginning and end
Time is birth and death
Time is bloom and decay
Time is the pendulum of Duality

Eternity is NOWNESS forever
All is now
Infinity is HERENESS everywhere
All places here
ISNESS be without form without name without end
The beginning be without end

Time be temporal and finite
In time all is subject to death
This includes all existence in materiality

Soul must practice patience
As the Creator expresses ITS capacity
And infinite willingness to endure
The separation
The Creator waits patiently for spirit's return
Yours and mine

Soul needs to be patient with Soul

So many made at different lights sound fountain
 eruptions
On the road to GOD we help each other

By Nolan Luke, (Narendar Puri)Naga Baba

Although eternity is infinite and unending
The Creator is the event attraction and sunrise horizon
Though in eternity Soul must become invisible
In order to continue progress on the road to the Creator
Spirit drops its visible true form of Soul
On the way to being itself without form
The spiritual thirst and hunger for the Creator
That motivates Soul the formless spirit the poet
Ever onward and ever upward
Into finer regions and planes of existence
Leading closer to the origin source of all
Reflected on each and every Plane in existence

The Creator is at the center of everything
Thus the Creator is within and everywhere
The zero point center of every solar sun
Galaxy and universe in the multiverse

We are easily distracted by outer forms
And often do not see the Creator watching us
So we might forget its constant presence in our life
Maya the near perfect illusion that we live within
Like a dream everything and the people are real
Our physical manifestation crosses the river Lethe
We forget
We learn again names for GOD
And from deep inside we remember
We find GOD within ourselves
Forever the focus and attention of our existence
GOD leads us back to itself
As seen and unseen Formlessness

7-09-13

By Nolan Luke, (Narendar Puri)Naga Baba

A DIVE INTO NOTHINGNESS

I Soul as invisible formless spirit light
Did from the rim of the whirlpool
Fling myself down into the dark center of Nothingness
Of the Sugmad Vortex spinning churning whirling
To say I lost myself falling into Nothingness
Describes what I can recall

The surface of Nothingness has no splash
No film no membrane to yield
Into nothingness I fell into non existence
Voidness is much like oblivion and emptiness
In such a state of annihilation was I

Spirit and Soul consciousness requires creation and manifestation
Consciousness in that VOID unmanifestness
Is completely out of sync with existence

The unmanifest unknown unseen unheard Creator
Is beyond our experience and awareness and ken
Yet in Nothingness I detect nonexistence not any thing no deity
Zilch nada nothing here but me
A warm tear fallen into snow

Yet I continue still to exist somewhere somehow
Here is back before the advent of Creation

Consciousness is not extinguished by nonexistence

Consciousness can survive everything and
    nothingness forever

Suddenly in the black emptiness Thunder
Bright light
Sound so loud I was deaf and blind
A geyser exploded
I was a note flowing in a stream singing
Me and a gazillion instant new spirits made out of
    nothing
Flash into the manifest creation
I be the same
Except where I have changed in the NOTHINGNESS
7-10-13

By Nolan Luke, (Narendar Puri)Naga Baba

SPIRIT LIFETIME

Spirit is created to exist forever
Spirit cannot be killed
And is not subject to extinction
Spirit is the power cell of everything living
Spirit light is the scaffolding though formless
That the Soul body light form covers
Soul body light is visible
On all the Planes of existence
In eternity and below in time and materiality
Soul light can be seen in the physical multiverses and worlds
Astral Causal Mental Etheric planes and their worlds
Soul light is the outer cover layer
Over formless spirit consciousness

Spirit must dress to go outside
Formless spirit is like being naked
And dressing in the cold early morning darkness
A first layer of silk
A second layer of polyester
A third layer of wool
A forth layer of fleece
A fifth layer of down

Spirit conscious light is ready for the great outdoors
Wrapped in Soul wrapped in Etheric wrapped in Mental
Wrapped in Causal wrapped in Astral wrapped in Physical
Spirit returns to physical life time and time again

Arriving through birth leaving through death
Time after time again and again
7-10-13

By Nolan Luke, (Narendar Puri)Naga Baba

BEAUTY

I see her face
Through my closed eyes

Modest though she be
I see her smile as I look at her
I never promised to not look
I said I would close my eyes
While she showered in the rain

Her beauty overwhelms me
Her curves curl my mind and thoughts
Until I no longer have linear thinking

She dances naked in the rain
I intuit the lights and colors of her movements
I see within her even greater beauty
Spiritual light of a Goddess

Dwelling in the sensuality of flesh
A divine gift to any Goddess of the esoteric realms
That even a brief appearance being seen by mortals
Supercharges the Goddess and GOD

Beauty inspires love making truth real
The truth of attraction and racing heartbeats
The truth of feeling the heart and mind as Soul

SPIRITUAL IMAGERY

The truth of being somehow familiar
Perhaps in another lifetime
The truth of thought anticipating beauty
The truth of intuition flashing her beauty
The truth of self knowing beauty

The divinity of lovemaking
Soul to Soul
Light to light
Is synergy energy and spiritual imagery

After the unmanifest formless one
Came into manifestation
The center point of Creation began
Extending ever outward ever downward
Into Planes of existences of ever greater densities and
       solar gravity and physical matter

Love goodness generosity joy elation gladness
Sweet nectar perfect lighting perfect music
Of course intercourse happened
Thus Creation came into being manifested NOW

The Creator is making love to us eternally
All is sustained by love unconditional

By Nolan Luke, (Narendar Puri)Naga Baba

Love creates nourishes renews washes and blesses a being
Love arouses Soul and Goddesses and God into the physical activity
The physical material existence is then blessed
By a supercharged Goddess flowing love into the world

7-11-13

INTO THE WIND

Just as baby birds
Eventually jump off the nest
Into the larger world around them
So does Soul eventually jump off the earth
Into the extraordinary world within

Soul can outgrow the physical material worlds
Soon after experiencing the reality above time
Above matter above physical space
In timelessness we get a measure of eternity
Seven tenths of a second of time
Spent in the timelessness of heavenly regions
Is like spending four and a half hours
On a walk around visit
On some high upper Plane of immaterial existence

The material worlds run on time
Time is the clockwork mechanism
Time is not just for calculation and measurement
Time is not straight
Time may run a long duration
But time curves
Time does not run in a straight line
Time is the material reflection
Of the Sugmad Vortex spinning churning whirlpooling
Formless far above us here on earth

By Nolan Luke, (Narendar Puri)Naga Baba

Flexing our toes on our tip toes on the very edge of the world
All while sitting still in the center
Looking within for that door that opens above material time
And the great leap forward into the BANI wind
7-13-13

THE DAUGHTER

Who is she
Ah yes a wind spirit from a Goddess Temple
But first let me in secret
Confide that I have become acquainted recently
With the Wind's daughter
I do not know where there be the other eight daughters
But I have met this daughter of the wind
I know her secret name
But I will not tell
A beautiful wind is she
When she breezes by gently
And caresses me lovingly
I forget she is immaterial to the eyes
Yet when she giggles
When she sighs
I so want to call her name
Tell her I see you here
When she whispers in my ear her sweet heart feelings
I want to kiss her
And just as I lean to do so
The air billows
She is gone in a change of direction
True daughter of the wind
She wears the perfume of late summer evening
And nothing else

By Nolan Luke, (Narendar Puri)Naga Baba

When she dances she moves faster than silk
Here is cosmic nature so effortlessly
Hard to imagine
She spent the last thousand years as am air bubbly
Tricked trapped forced into a box and sealed
I happened to come upon the box and thought I heard
       a voice inside

THE BOX

No screws nails or dowels
The wood box had been sealed a long time ago
Its size was able to hold a human head or artifact
Of a priestess when travelling
Maybe there was something ancient inside
But it held something else
I could hear a voice inside
How much? I asked the couple holding the yard sale
It doesn't open or anything at all she said
It's just a box
So I guess we could let it go cheap
Say five dollars
It doesn't have a key cause there is no lock
It could make a good door stop or something like that
Because of that little voice inside the box
I bought the box and brought it home
I read a lot of material on old fashioned woodcraft
      and ancient technology
And figured out the composition
And compounds of the sealant
Pretty much mixed up the solution there on the spot
Applied it dabbing all along the lid and the hinges
And little by little the seals dissolved
Hours it took
All the while I could hear the voice clearly
Turns out this wind spirit was a breath that entered

By Nolan Luke, (Narendar Puri)Naga Baba

A Goddess child at birth found each lifetime
To be the living temple representative of the Goddess
The Goddess lived in the world through the child
The child acquired Grace and Wisdom
She the voice of the Goddess
She shared her beauty with the Goddess
She embodied the Goddess

THE AIREY TALE

Men attacked the Goddess temple
The Goddess temple fell
Palace intrigue men conniving men dressed in the women's priestess clothes robes and shoes
Poison splashed and the men tool over
Spells devils and evil intent entered worship
Betrayal on a grand scale
She fell into a stupor into sleep into a coma
Her final breath captured
And sealed within the box air tight
The girl slave lifetime after lifetime
While the voice was held in the box somewhere else where
The solution dissolved the sealant
The lid of the box opened
At first the air in the box was still
Stale fragrances rose sandalwood frankincense
I could smell
I had thought of closing the box
There was nothing to see
The box was empty to all appearances
Until I could hear her awakening
She might have been startled by the light
I explained how I found and opened the box
She told me her story
I waited
Then as a cool breeze she rose out of the box

By Nolan Luke, (Narendar Puri)Naga Baba

Until she was standing before me
Her body outline swirls of air
I see her and see through her at the same time
She is beauty she is wind
She is seen she is unseen

THE BREEZES PASS BY

Here on this warm July evening
I feel her on my skin
Touching me as she does
And then she is gone again
Like the wind she is
Except now she has her voice back
She flies around dancing and speaking loud
I say she might as well be singing
The future is here now
If one elects to use it
Time bends curves even runs back on itself
Like a root following found water traces
Time moves forward without direction
We can bend time
We can stretch time
Time like the wind can be compressed
And so now the Daughter of the Wind is free
When she is away all is so still
When she is here with me the air is enlivened
I breathe more easily
And when I squint my eyes
I can almost see her
Unseen beauty naked and revealed
This being a secret tell no one
What you hear this evening
When the wind is softly near
And the scent of rose and jasmine is in the air
7-13-13

By Nolan Luke, (Narendar Puri)Naga Baba

THE GODDESS

See what she does to me
My senses are reversed
Inside is outside
The future is flowing backwards
History is tomorrow
The long ago is now
That which is coming is ahead and already passed
I can barely see the moment I am in
Maybe I have gone crazy
Maybe I have gone mad
I walked into her temple
I saw her golden shiny face
I do not remember if I fell to my knees
But I did surrender my heart
I gave my love on first sight
Her voice set my ears to ringing
I found myself in her embrace
Which plane of existence were we
They all seem a blur
I am sure of the physical meeting
I breathed in her perfume
I felt her gaze
I remembered across lifetimes
Her eyes seeing me again
Here in her Inner Sanctum,
Where wishes are granted
And blessings are bestowed
All because of this Goddess I love
7-13-13

CHAPTER FIVE

THE PHYSICAL MATERIAL – LIBERATION – REINCARNATION

By Nolan Luke, (Narendar Puri)Naga Baba

A BUTTERFLY

A butterfly
Fluttering on warm Indian Summer breezes
Appeared under the eaves
For a moment
She was a beautiful Monarch
Perhaps on her way to Mexico
Alone unafraid curious
On her life journey
From an egg laid underneath a leaf
Into a ravenous caterpillar
Eating itself into a transformative dream sleep
The trance a Baba a Yogi a Holy Man Holy Woman
    Goes into meditation into Rejuvenation
        Transformation
Becoming the potential already within one's true self
The dream is as important as the self-effort
Dreaming vividly utilizes creative energy
    What dreams do caterpillars experience when
        sleeping
Do they daydream while eating while dozing
Perhaps they know their true nature
Some of the most beautiful women
Were ugly duckling plain Janes in their younger years
Yet the beauty was there though perhaps unseen
So when next you see a caterpillar
Take a close slow observance
Do not disturb the world you see
Every life tells a story to God and Goddess
This one the potential of transformation
10-12-13

SAMADHI

Samadhi transforms the already Enlightened
Into the true spiritual identity
The true spiritual form
The true spiritual light
The true spiritual Consciousness Awareness

The object of her contemplation the Sat Nam
The eternal true light form of the Formless Isness

I noticed starting December 20th, 2012
Diane Gail was spending her time
Her eyes rolled upward
Looking into her Tisra Til

She would blink and come out of contemplation
Engage in conversation eat interact smiling
And would then reenter contemplation
She was crystal clear calm serene happy
Warm loving giving
And she kept trying to tell me she was leaving
I would not hear it she was in her best health in years
I am sorry I did not listen
I did not notice her siddha displays
I would not have let her go if it were up to me
She entered Samadhi soul conscious aware
She attained her Jivan Mukti as a Spiritual Traveller
She left while I was not looking
On that we differed

By Nolan Luke, (Narendar Puri)Naga Baba

I celebrate her total liberation from Samsara
I am blessed to have been a witness

THE SQUIRREL EXISTENTIAL LEAP

Those pesky squirrels again
I halted their assaults on the Goddess fig tree
Sent them both back to jump on one of the palm trees
And all of this afternoon I kept them treed
Until one of them took a flying leap
From the very top of the green
Maybe it was going for the redwood across the driveway
Maybe it was going for a further palm tree
I don't know
It said nothing before the leap
Easily a hundred feet to the blacktop asphalt
As it was falling headfirst
I thought wow I've never seen anything like this
It was picking up speed and falling
And took awhile
As I watched it clear the width of the driveway
Sixteen feet wide from the tree
Another seven feet equals twenty three foot leap the jump
Headfirst tail following
It did not come down horizontal
Like a gliding flying squirrel
This is a regular gray tree squirrel bushy tail
I think I caught its eye glance on the way down
Paws forward like a high dive into a pool of water
As the squirrel got closer to the ground
My neck tensed I gritted my teeth

By Nolan Luke, (Narendar Puri)Naga Baba

Six feet from the ground I sensed Nowness time standing still
Then I heard it struck asphalt then I heard it scamper away

I said out loud
What the
I walked over to the palm trees where I could see
Where it hit the ground
On the other side of the driveway
There were three small piles of sand
The squirrel hit the middle pile of sand
The larger of the three
But not larger by much
So did the squirrel intend the outcome
Or was it a case of squirrel luck
There is no dead body injured body
No fur and no sign of it anywhere
Upon even closer inspection
Those were no sand piles but was dirt that was solid
    as clods
And what was annoying was that it gave a chatter
From the safety of the hedgerow
Cheeky attitude arrogant disposition
But then if you know tree squirrels
This may be no surprise
Yet
That leap to the ground was incredible
For an ordinary tree squirrel
But then everything and everyone
Has the same spiritual potential already in the spirit
Animating the atoms of existence with life
    consciousness
10-14-13

By Nolan Luke, (Narendar Puri)Naga Baba

THE DANCE OF LIBERATION

We tend to assume or believe that the Creator
Is far far far away from the material planes of existence
And it would seem so
Except for the rare utterances out of nothingness
ITS humor is the truth of intimacy with the creation
IT is the empty space between all things
IT is the unseen behind the blinding light
Are we not all in God
Is not the all God
Diversity the beautiful
Individual the Consciousness
Individualized Spirit beyond form and visibility
We be though still in the body living on earth
So the Formless Isness
The whirlpool and fountain
Manifesting the Unmanifest
Is also at onement with all and everything
Creation is our training school campus
We have been given the gift the task of consciousness
The awakening of the true self
The actualization living as the true self here and now
Recognizing Self Realizing the truth of identity
Each Soul slaying its own beast of ignorance and destruction
Just like God like Goddess
Dancing on the corpse of one's own ignorance and negativity

The dance of liberation
Free from the shackles of the Samsara
Moksha from the endless rounds of lifetimes

By Nolan Luke, (Narendar Puri)Naga Baba

LIFETIME AFTER LIFETIME

Lifetime after lifetime
Without a reminder of home
Soul can forget
Who they actually be
Why they are here
And where are they going from here
Or will they simply continue
To return again to be from here
In simply a brand new body again
Reincarnation is administered fairly
The afterlife is fair due to reactions
One's own past actions can cause suffering
The afterlife is like a time out
Note: Do not judge others do not judge yourself
For if you are to be judged leave it to the Lords of Karma
They are more lenient than the self that is judgmental
The afterlife is where we pay back our actions on others by feeling their suffering pain
And pay down the karma charged
On the Cosmic Karma Debit Card
The afterlife is not time out from Samsara
Therefore it is time for strategy to improve toward enlightenment
Many at birth forget their given promise to remember God everyday
Many forget who they truly be

Not in control of themselves
Soul is subject to its own ego the mind
Ego fraudulently swipes the identity card
And Soul is burdened to pay unable to leave Samsara
Due to the debt balance ever increasing
Lifetime after lifetime

By Nolan Luke, (Narendar Puri)Naga Baba

DIVINE MOTHER

Mother
As seen by the new born baby
Is Divine
Divine Mother
Giving forth birth nourishment guidance and wisdom

Mother Dear
As seen by that same baby sixty five years later
Mother is one with the Divine Mother
Mother represents the Divine Mother
Mother personifies the Divine Mother

Mother
When you smile
You let that light shine bright
When you laugh
That light can be heard

I know what so many see and hear in you
I love how much you are loved
I understand them loving your Beingness
You connect with each Soul individually
You cast a light unseen except to spirit
Lucky me first born and number one son

My love my blessings to you Mother
My well wishes and many happy birthdays to come

I say on your eighty first birthday and getting younger

By Nolan Luke, (Narendar Puri)Naga Baba

RAIN

Clouds filled the sky
Beneath the Blue
The wind blew cold
The rain sprinkled
The downpour came
And washed the layers of dust
Off the fig tree leaves

THE SPIRITUAL TRAVELLER'S GUIDEBOOK TO ETERNITY

INSTALLMENTS published 2017 – 2018

Part 1 – With Odes to My Beloved

Part 2 – The Satta Loka

Part 3 - The Goddess

Part 4 - Eternity

www.ingramcontent.com/pod-product-compliance
Lightning Source LLC
Chambersburg PA
CBHW022113040426
42450CB00006B/683